THE AMERICANA SONGBOOK:
CLASSIC AMERICAN ROOTS MUSIC

Cover art by Levin Pfeufer

Cherry Lane Music Company
Director of Publications/Project Editor: Mark Phillips

ISBN 1-57560-744-1

Copyright © 2005 Cherry Lane Music Company
International Copyright Secured   All Rights Reserved

Visit our website at www.cherrylane.com

C O N T E N T S

Alison

Words and Music by
Elvis Costello

way you look, I un - der - stand that you are not im - pressed.
leave your pret - ty fin - gers ly - ing in the wed - ding cake?

But I heard you let that lit - tle friend of mine __ I'll bet
You used to hold him right in your hand. __

take off your par - ty dress. __
he took all he could take. __

I'm not gon - na get too sen - ti - men - tal like those
Some - times I wish that I could stop you from talk - ing when I

oth - er stick - y val - en - tines, ___
hear the sil - ly things that you say. ___

'cause I don't know if you ___ are lov - ing some - bod - y. I
I think some - bod - y bet - ter put out the big light, 'cause I

on - ly know ___ it is - n't mine. ___
can't stand to ___ see you this way. ___

Al - i - son, ___ I know ___ this world ___ is kill -

ing you. ___ Oh, _____ Al - i - son, ___

my aim ___ is true. ___

My aim ___ is true. ___

Repeat and fade

Can't Let Go

Written by
Randy Weeks

Told me, ba - by, one more time; ___ don't make me sit all a -
I got a can - dle and it burns so bright __ in my win - dow
Turn off trou - ble like you turn off a light. Went off and left me; it

D.S. al Coda

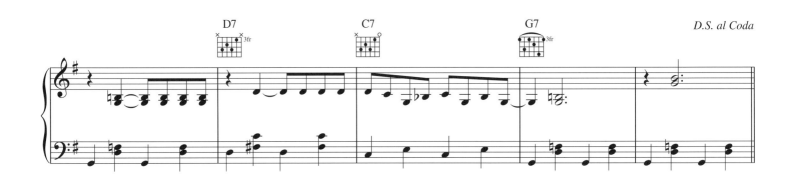

It's o - ver. I know ___ it but I can't let

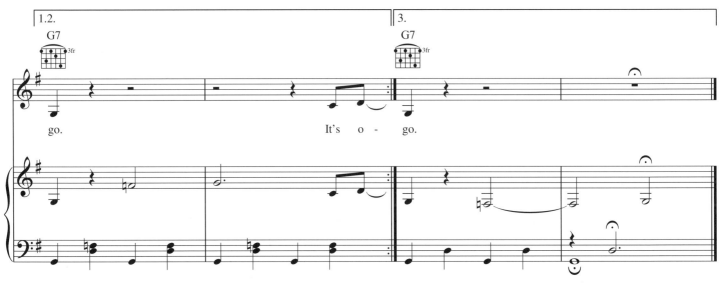

go. It's o - go.

Chuck E's in Love

Words and Music by
Rickie Lee Jones

Chuck E's ___ in love. _____

Chuck E's ___ in love. ___ Chuck E's ___ in

love. I don't be - lieve _____ what you're say - ing to me. ___ This is some - thing that

I got - ta see. Is he here? Look in the pool - hall. Is he here? ___

Additional Lyrics

2. He learn all of the lines,
   And every time, he don't stutter when he talk.
   And it's true! It's true!
   He sure is acquired a cool and inspired sorta jazz when he walk.
   Where's his jacket and his old blue jeans?
   If this ain't healthy, it is some kinda clean. *(To Chorus)*

3. I'll tell you what, I saw him.
   He was sittin' behind us down at the Pantages.
   And whatever it is that he's got up his sleeve,
   I hope it isn't contagious.
   What's her name?
   Is that her there? *(To Coda)*

Cigarettes and Chocolate Milk

Words and Music by
Rufus Wainwright

lit - tle bit harm - ful for ____ me. And then there's those oth - er things, ___
lit - tle old doll ____ with a frown. You got to keep in the game, ___

which for sev - 'ral rea - sons we won't
main - tain - ing mys - tique while fac - ing

men - tion. _____ Ev - 'ry - thing a - bout 'em is a
for - ward. _____ I sug - gest a read - ing of "a

lit - tle bit strang - er, a lit - tle bit hard - er, a
les - son in tight - ropes," or "surf - ing your high____ hopes," or

so bro - ken - heart - ed.

Still there's not a show on my back, __

holes ___ or a friend-ly in-ter-ven-tion. ___ I'm just a

lit-tle bit ___ heir-ess, a lit-tle bit I - rish, a

lit-tle bit ___ Tow-er of Pi - sa when-

ev - er I see ___ you, ___ so

please be kind _____ if I'm a mess.

molto rit.

mp
a tempo

Cig - a - rettes and choc - o - late milk. ____

rit.

Freely

Cig - a - rettes and choc - o - late _____ milk. ____

Closer to Fine

Words and Music by
Emily Saliers

give me in - sight be - tween black __ and white. _____

And the best thing __ you've ev - er done __ for me _____ is to help __

__ me take __ my life __ less se - ri - ous - ly. ____ It's on - ly life af - ter all. __

To Coda ⊕

To next strain

2. Well sank it. I'm crawl - ing on __ your shores.

I

less I seek ___ my source ___ for some ___ de - fin - i - tive, ___ the clo - ser ___ I ___
(less   I   seek   my   source)

am to fine. _____ The clos - er ___ I am to fine. _____

3. I _____

Instrumental interlude

D.S. al Coda

4. I

28

Additional Lyrics

2. Well, darkness has a hunger that's insatiable, and lightness has a call that's hard to hear.
   I wrap my fear around me like a blanket.
   I sailed my ship of safety till I sank it.
   I'm crawling on your shores.

3. I went to the Doctor of Philosophy with a poster of Rasputin and a beard down do his knee.
   He never did marry or see a B - Grade movie.
   He graded my performance, he said he could see through me.
   I spent four years prostrate to the higher mind, got my paper and I was free.

4. I stopped by a bar at three A.M. to seek solace in a bottle, or possibly a friend.
   I woke up with a headache like my head against a board, twice as cloudy as I'd been the night before.
   And I went in seeking clarity.

Don't Know Why

Words and Music by
Jesse Harris

Some - thing has ___ to ___ make ___ you run. ___

Eight Miles High

Words and Music by Roger McGuinn,
David Crosby and Gene Clark

Feels Like Home

Words and Music by
Randy Newman

back where I be - long. _____ It feels like _ I'm

all _____ the way _____ back where I be - long. _____

rall.

a tempo

rall.

From a Distance

Words and Music by
Julie Gold

voice of ev - 'ry man.   From a
songs of ev - 'ry

man.   God_ is watch-ing us,___ God_ is watch-ing us,   God_ is

watch-ing us   from a dis-tance.___

46

Hickory Wind

Words and Music by
Gram Parsons and Bob Buchanan

Hummingbird

Words and Music by
Leon Russell

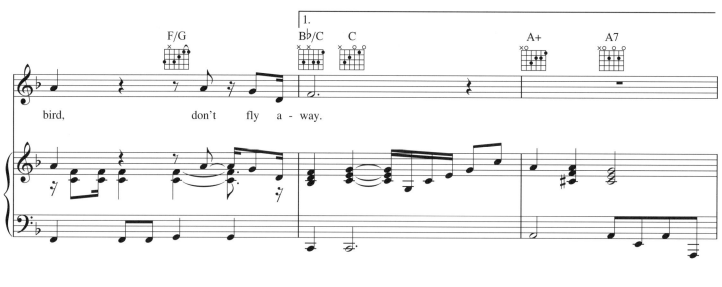

I Can't Make You Love Me

Words and Music by
Mike Reid and Allen Shamblin

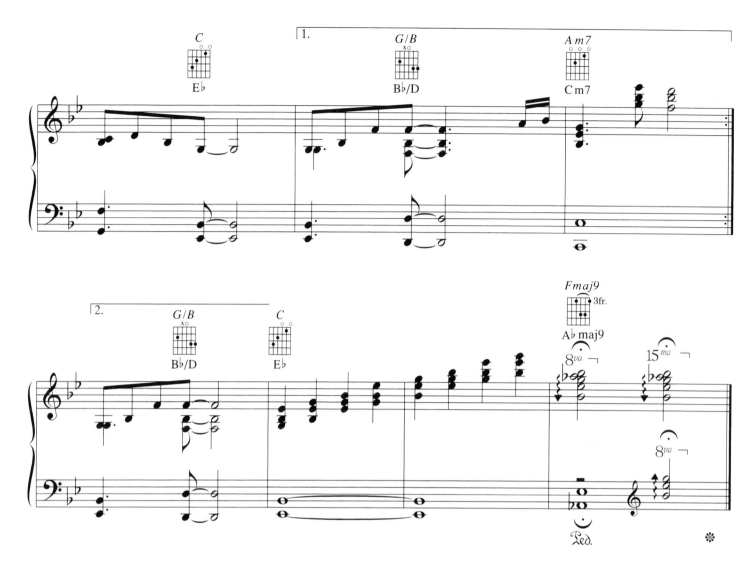

Additional Lyrics

2. I'll close my eyes, then I won't see
The love you don't feel when you're holdin' me.
Mornin' will come and I'll do what's right.
Just give me till then to give up this fight.
And I will give up this fight. *(To Chorus)*

I Will Remember You

Theme from THE BROTHERS McMULLEN

Words and Music by Sarah McLachlan,
Seamus Egan and Dave Merenda

your warmth up-on ____ me. I wan-na be the one. ___
ing in - side or we ___ can't be heard.
gave me ev - 'ry - thing you had, oh, you gave me light. ___

I will re - mem - ber ___ you. ___

Will you re - mem - ber ___ me? ___ Don't let your life ___

pass ___ you by. ___ Weep not for _____ the

Jealousy

Words and Music by
Natalie Merchant

Moderately

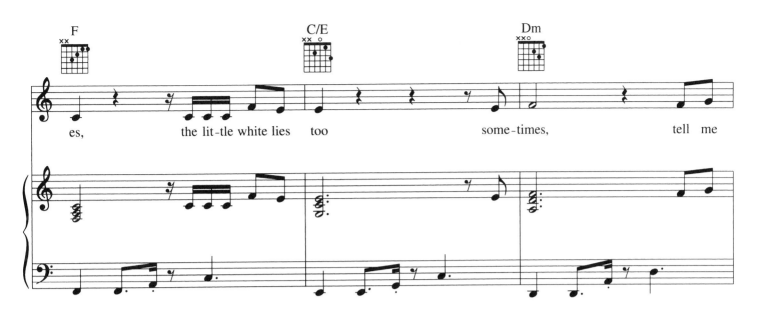

es, the lit-tle white lies too some-times, tell me

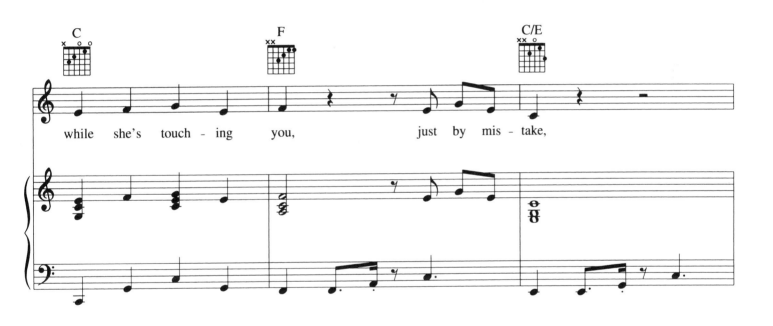

while she's touch - ing you, just by mis - take,

ac - cid - ent - 'lly do you say my name?

poco rit.

p

Kind & Generous

Words and Music by
Natalie Merchant

Oh,_____ I want to thank you for so man-y gifts___ you gave___ with love,___ with ten-der-ness.___ I want to thank you.___

I want to thank you for your gen-er-os-i-ty,___ the love___ and the hon-es-ty___ that you gave___ me.

74

L.A. Song

Words and Music by
Beth Hart

and she tried __ and she tried __ and she tried, __ but noth-ing's clear __ in a bar __ full of flies, __ so she takes __
and she cried, __ and she cried __ and she cried. __ She cried so long __ her tears __ ran dry. __ And she laughed __

and she takes, __ she takes and she takes. __ She un-der-stands __ when she gives __ it a-way. __ She says:
and she laughed, __ she laughed and she laughed, __ 'cause she knew she __ was nev-er __ com-in' back. __ She said:

Man, I got-ta get out-ta this town. __ Man, I got-ta get out-ta this pain. __
Man, I'm gon-na get out-ta this town. __ Man, I'm gon-na get out-ta this pain. __

Man, I got-ta get out-ta this town, __ out-ta this town, __ and out-ta L. A. __
Man, I'm gon-na get out-ta this town, __ out-ta this town, __ and out-ta L. A. __

77

Let It Roll

Words and Music by
Billy Payne, Paul Barrere
and Martin Kibbee

sail - in' through_ her home- town coun - try - side._
sit my ba - by right_ down by_ my side._
reach be - neath_ my big_ old steer - ing wheel.

A

Move on o - ver, stand_ a - side,_ my cruise_ con - trol's_ in o -
Where the rub - ber hits_ the road_ this rig_ don't dig_ no o -
Dy - na flow, _ pow - er glide,_ bored _ and stroked,_ I'm sat -

G   E

ver - drive, _
ver - load. _   need to take_ my ba - by for a _
is - fied _   Come on   and let_ my ba - by ride._
                  when I   take my ba - by for_ a ride._

E   F♯m7/E   G°/E

_ ride.)
                         Ooh, _ she's like a smooth.

Play 15 times
Last time D.S. al Coda

(Instrumental solo ad lib)

Coda

Play 3 times

Little Good-byes

Words and Music by
Kristyn Osborn, Kenny Greenberg,
and Jason Deere

one last min-ute of my ___ time in this mess I left be-hind. _____

When you come home to-night ___ and turn on the light, ___

don't you be ___ sur-prised ___ to find ___ my lit-tle good-

byes, _____ my lit-tle good-
Emp-ty hang-ers by the clos-et door, ___ lip-stick tube on the bath-room floor, ___

And if you're won - d'rin' when you're gon - na hear __ from me, ___ well, take a

real good look a - round, __ boy, and it won't be hard to see. ___

When you come home to - night __ and turn on the light, __

don't you be __ sur - prised __ to find __ my lit - tle good -

Pancho and Lefty

Written by Townes Van Zandt

out of kind - ness, I___ sup-pose."___

1st time, D.S. (take 2nd ending);
2nd time, D.S. (take 2nd ending;
repeat Chorus) al Coda

To Coda ⊕   𝄋

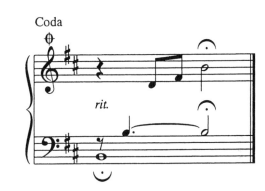

Coda

rit.

Additional Lyrics

2. Pancho was a bandit, boys.
   His horse was fast as polished steel.
   He wore his gun outside his pants
   For all the honest world to feel.
   Pancho met his match, you know,
   On the deserts down in Mexico.
   And nobody heard his dyin' words.
   But that's the way it goes. *(To Chorus)*

3. Well Lefty, he can't sing the blues
   All night long like he used to.
   The dust that Pancho bit down south
   Ended up in Lefty's mouth.
   The day they laid poor Pancho low
   Lefty split for Ohio.
   And where he got the bread to go.
   Aw, there ain't nobody knows. *(To Chorus)*

4. Well, the poets tell how Pancho fell.
   Lefty's livin' in a cheap hotel.
   The desert's quiet and Cleveland's cold.
   So the story ends, we're told.
   Pancho needs your prayers, it's true,
   Save a few for Lefty too.
   He just did what he had to do.
   And now he's growin' old. *(To Chorus)*

San Francisco Bay Blues

Words and Music by
Jesse Fuller

Sit-tin' down and look-in' through my back door Won-d'rin' which way to go, ___

Wo-man I'm so cra - zy 'bout she don't want me no more.

Think I'll take me a freight train, Be-cause I'm feel-in' blue,

Ride all the way to the end of the line, ___ Think-in' on-ly of you.

16 Days

Written by
Ryan Adams

wed - ding   ring. _____
pol - o - gy. _____

Got six - teen days. ___

Fif - teen ___ of those ___ are nights. ___   Can't sleep ___ when the bed - sheet fights ___

its way ___ back to your side. _____   Well, the ghost ___

___ has got me run - nin',   the ghost ___ has got me run - nin'
(The ghost ___ has got me run - nin'.)   (The ghost ___

mf

a - way ___ from you, ___ a - way ___ from you, ___ a - way. ___
___ has got me run - nin'.)

Well, the ghost ___ has got me run - nin', (The ghost ___

well, the ghost ___ has got me run - nin' a - way ___
___ has got me run - nin'.) (The ghost ___ has got me run - nin'.)

___ from you, ___ a - way ___ from you, ___ a - way. ___
Got

Sunshine
(Go Away Today)

Written by
Jonathan Edwards

Moderately

Sun-shine go __ a - way to-day, __ I don't feel much __ like __
Sun-shine go __ a - way to-day, __ I don't feel much __ like __

danc - in'. __ Some man's gone __ and tried to run my __ life. __ He
danc - in'. __ Some man's gone __ and tried to run my __ life. __ He

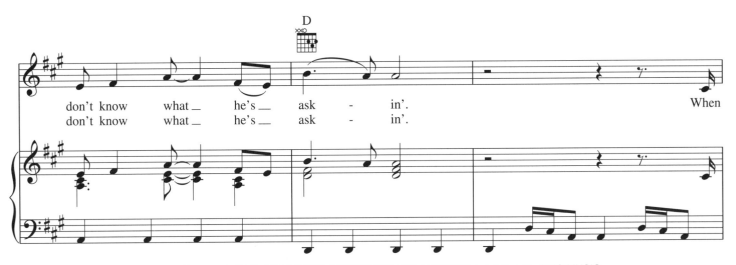

don't know what __ he's __ ask - in'. When
don't know what __ he's __ ask - in'.

he tells me __ I bet-ter get in line, __ I can't hear what __ he's __
Work-in' starts __ to make me won-der where __ the fruits of what __ I do are
Sun-shine, come __ on back an-oth-er day, __ I prom-ise you __ I'll be __

say - in'. When I grow up, __ I'm gon-na make it mine, __ or
go - in'. He says in love __ and war __ all is fair, __ but
sing - in'. This old world, __ she's gon-na turn a - round; __

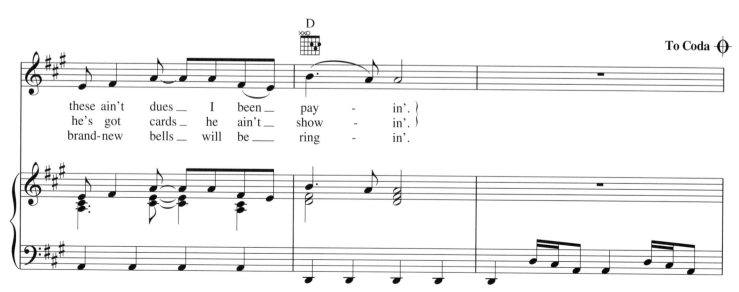

these ain't dues __ I been pay - in'.
he's got cards __ he ain't show - in'.
brand-new bells __ will be __ ring - in'.

To Coda ⊕

Thing Called Love
(Are You Ready for This Thing Called Love)

Words and Music by
John Hiatt

111

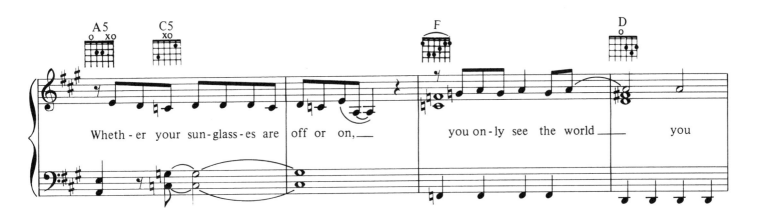

Wheth - er your sun-glass-es are off or on,___ you on-ly see the world___ you

D.S. al Coda

N.C.

make.

Coda

Are you read -y for it? Are you read-y for the thing called love?___

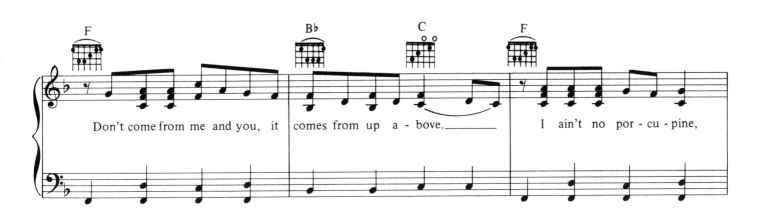

Don't come from me and you, it comes from up a - bove.___ I ain't no por-cu-pine,

take off your kid   gloves._   Are you read - y   for it?

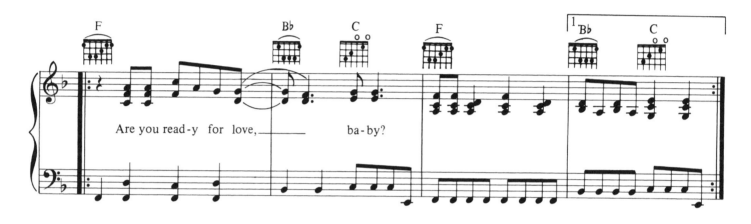

Are you read -y for love,_____   ba-by?

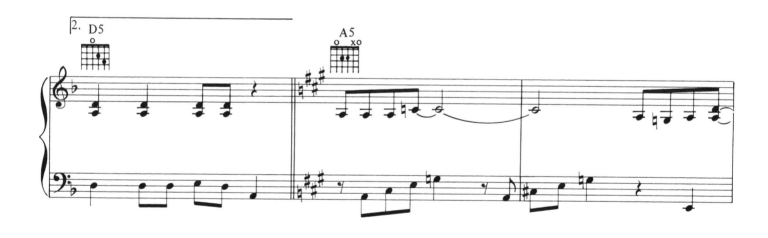

Turn! Turn! Turn!
(To Everything There Is a Season)

Words from the Book of Ecclesiastes
Adaptation and Music by Pete Seeger

Walking in Memphis

Words and Music by
Marc Cohn

The Way We Make a Broken Heart

Written by John Hiatt

131

The Weight

By J.R. Robertson

1. I pulled in-to Na - za-reth, was feel-in' 'bout half - past dead.
(Verses 2-5. see block lyrics)

I just need some place _ where I can lay _ my head. _____

"Hey, mis-ter can you tell me ___ where a man might find a bed?" ___

He just grinned and shook my hand, ___ "No" was all ___ he said.

Take a load off Fan - ny,   take a load for free. ___

Take a load off Fan - ny   and ___
                                                and ___
                                            and ___ you

133

Verse 2:

I picked up my bag, I went looking for a place to hide
When I saw Carmen and the Devil walking side by side
I said "Hey, Carmen, come on, let's go down town."
She said, "I gotta go but my friend can stick around."

Take a load off Fanny etc.

Verse 3:

Go down, Miss Moses, there's nothing you can say
It's just ol' Luke and Luke's waiting on the judgement day
"Well, Luke my friend, what about young Anna Lee?"
He said "Do me a favour son, won't you stay
    and keep Anna Lee Company?"

Take a load off Fanny etc.

Verse 4:

Crazy Chester followed me and he caught me in the fog
He said "I will fix your rack if you'll take Jack, my dog."
I said "Wait a minute Chester, you know a peaceful man."
He said "That's O.K. boy, won't you feed him when you can."

Take a load off Fanny etc.

Verse 5:

Catch a cannonball now, to take me down the line
My bag is sinking low and I do believe it's time
To get back to Miss Fanny, you know she's the only one
Who sent me here with her regards for everyone.

Take a load off Fanny etc.

When I Was a Boy

Written by
Dar Williams

And I don't know __ how I __ sur - vived.
And I know things __ have got - ta change.
And I __ could al - ways cry.

I guess I knew __ the tricks __ that all __ boys __ knew.
They got pills __ to sell; __ they've got im - plants __ to put in; __ they got im -
Now e - ven when __ I'm a - lone I sel - dom __ do.

plants __ to re - move. __

And __ you __ can walk __
But __ I __ am not __
And __ I __ have lost __

Where Have All the Cowboys Gone?

Words and Music by
Paula Cole

Oh, _____ you get me read - y in your
don't you stay the eve - ning, kick
fi - n'lly sold the Chev - y when we

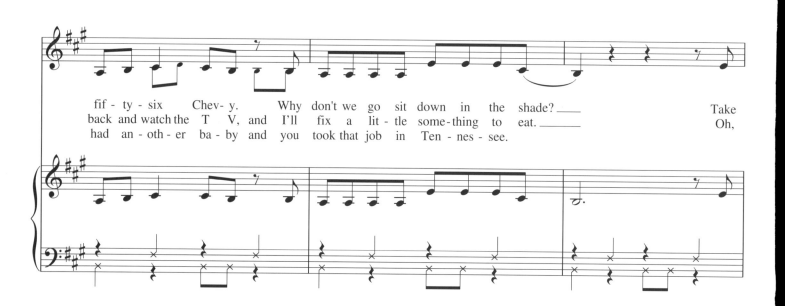

fif - ty - six Chev - y. Why don't we go sit down in the shade? _____ Take
back and watch the T V, and I'll fix a lit - tle some - thing to eat. _____ Oh,
had an - oth - er ba - by and you took that job in Ten - nes - see.

shel - ter on my front porch, the dan - de - li - on sun's scorch - in',
   I know your back hurts from work - in' on the trac - tor. How
made friends at the farm and you join 'em at the bar al - most

Why Walk When You Can Fly

Words and Music by
Mary Chapin Carpenter

Moderately

with pedal

A cappella

In this world there's a whole lot of trou-ble, ba-by; in this world there's a

whole lot of pain. In this world there's a whole lot of trou-ble, but a

whole lot of ground_____ to gain. Why take when you could be

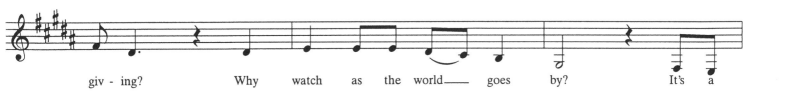

giv - ing?   Why   watch   as   the   world___   goes   by?   It's   a

hard e- nough life   to   be   liv - ing. Why   walk when you___ can   fly?

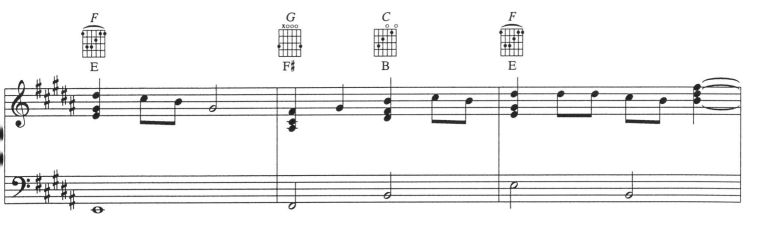

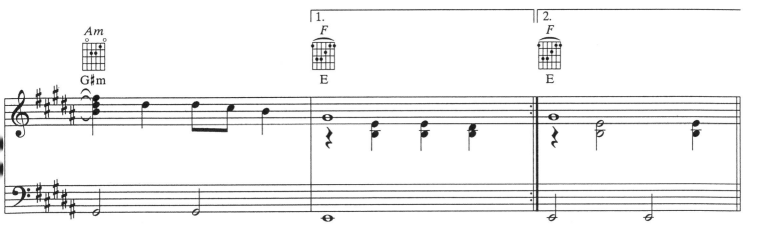

*Guitarists: Tune all strings down a half step.